THE A-TEAM PRESENTS...
Top Secret Mission #4

Lily Gets Bossy

Authored by
Courtney Butorac

Illustrations by
Emily Zieroth

Produced by PBL Consulting
936 NW 57th St
Seattle, WA 98107
www.sociallearning.org

Please contact
PBL Consulting at
info@pblconsulting.org
for more information.
Copyright 2016.
All rights reserved.

MW00956144

My name is Lily and I like to be in charge. When you are the boss, you get to go first, you get to choose the game and other people do what you say!

2

On Monday, when I was eating lunch in the cafeteria with Bella and Jack, I told them that we should eat our fruit first.

4

"Yeah," said Bella.
"Fruit is good for you.
So, we should
eat it first."

See, it was a
great idea!

5

On Tuesday, I was playing outside with my friends Sara and Lisa.

"Let's play family," I said. "I am the mom and you both are my daughters,"

6

Sara said she wanted to be the mom, but I reminded her that I was in charge, so I got to choose. And, we played the game my way.

On Wednesday, it was raining outside so we played inside for recess. I told Max we should play chess.

8

"I'm black!" I called. "You are always black!" Max whined. "Yeah, well I chose the game so I get to choose the color."

"Fine," he said.

We played and I beat him, as usual.

9

Thursday, Alex and I were outside playing a basketball game called HORSE.

"I'm going first!"
I shouted.

"But I wanted to go first!"
He said.

"Yeah, well, I called it,"
I told him.

Alex glared at me. "Oh fine, you can go first," Alex said.

And, we played the game my way.

11

On Friday, our teacher, Ms. Miller, gave us a project to do.

Our assignment was to work in groups of four, observing and taking notes on rocks.

As a group, we were supposed to decide who does each job.

"I will get the rocks. Bella will describe what they look like. Lisa will describe what they feel like and Sara will take notes," I explained.

"Hey, I want to get the rocks!" Lisa said.

"Yeah, and I want to feel them," Sara exclaimed.

"But this makes sense!" I said back to them.

"No, this isn't fair," Lisa replied. "You can't make all the decisions for the group! We have to decide together. That's what the teacher said."

13

My teacher told me that the kids were right, that we had to make the decision together, as a team.

"This is stupid!" I yelled and knocked the rocks off the table.

Ms. Miller gave me a look and sent me to the office.

That afternoon I met with my friendship group - the A Team. We get together to learn about social skills and to help each other when we have challenges with friends or in class.

Today, I had something to say.

"Ms. Corina, my friends are being mean to me,"
I complained. "That's because you are so bossy
and always want to be in charge," Alex said.

"But my ideas are good and people like it
when I am in charge!" I exclaimed.

"Bella, do you have something to
share?" Ms. Corina asked.

"Well, you always choose the game
and want to be first..." Bella quietly said.

17

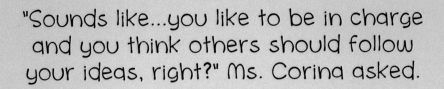

"Sounds like...you like to be in charge and you think others should follow your ideas, right?" Ms. Corina asked.

"Yes!" I said.

"But sometimes, your friends don't like your ideas or want to play a different game. Maybe they want to go first, even if you already called it."

"Yes!" I said again.

Have you noticed people's faces when you tell them what to do?" Ms. Corina asked me.

I thought of the kids' faces.
Some of them looked annoyed or disappointed.

"Well, I guess some of the kids don't like it when I'm in charge."

21

"One of the best ways to keep from being bossy is to try asking or suggesting. Instead of saying, 'give me that pen,' you can say, 'can I have that pen please?' Or instead of 'let's eat pizza,' you can say, 'maybe we can eat pizza' or 'what do you think if we eat pizza?'

When you are polite and use requesting language, you often get what you want, without others being upset with you and calling you bossy. Let's practice."

"Now, you may not always get what you want, but you might.

Plus, your friends will be much happier if you do it this way,"

Ms. Corina smiled at me. "Let's review a few more strategies."

24

BIG IDEA: Being a good leader means being a good listener, not just someone who tells everyone what to do.

So...

1. Use self-talk, which is like having a thought bubble above your head. Tell yourself, "I can't always be in charge. Sometimes, I need to let others lead." Or "my friends feel happy when they get to choose the game."

2. Use polite words, like "please" and "thank you"

3. Ask others for their ideas and be willing to try them.

4. Take turns being a leader.

Ms. Corina pulled me aside before I left.

"Lily, I want you to practice something with me."

I am going to give you a phrase. Let's practice changing it FROM being bossy TO being polite. Here we go:

'Let's play family today!'"

26

Ms. Corina's Room

"Do you want to play family today?" I asked.

"That's perfect, Lily! You shared your idea, but you did it politely so that your friends won't be upset about you being bossy."

She handed me an envelope. "Here is your Top Secret Mission. I want you to practice over the weekend and be ready to try it on Monday."

Monday came and I was ready to begin my mission.

My science group was meeting again to do the rock project. Ms. Miller reminded us that we needed to work together and make sure everyone's ideas were heard.

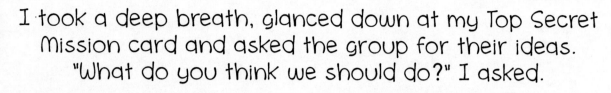

I took a deep breath, glanced down at my Top Secret Mission card and asked the group for their ideas. "What do you think we should do?" I asked.

Then, I listened carefully to what they had to say.

Lisa smiled and said, "I would like to get materials this time."

"That's a good idea," I said. "Is it okay if I get them tomorrow?"

"Yeah," Lisa said. "That makes sense."

I realized that being a good friend and teammate was more important than being the boss.

ABOUT THE AUTHOR

Courtney Butorac

Courtney Butorac has been supporting kids and adults with autism and also their families for 25 years as an elementary school special education teacher, preschool teacher, camp counselor and behavioral therapist. She has pioneered new ways to support social learning within her school district and is an enthusiastic member of a behavior and autism intervention team that engages district-wide to help teachers develop the knowledge and tools to support students with autism in their classrooms. Courtney has designed and facilitated powerful professional learning for educators that focuses on how to teach social skills to students with a broad range of disabilities and how to support behavioral needs in the classroom. Additionally, Courtney has guest lectured multiple times at the University of Washington's early childhood special education program.

Years ago, she and a group of her students with autism formed the A-Team friendship group to tackle the common social challenges facing her kids. These students helped inspire the "The A-Team Presents..." characters and book series.

Courtney has both a Master's Degree in early childhood special education and her Board Certification in Behavior Analysis (BCBA).

Courtney lives in Seattle with her husband, who is a fellow educator, and two young and energetic sons.

Explore more books about various social challenges in "The A-Team" book series!

Find useful, free resources on the web at sociallearning.org

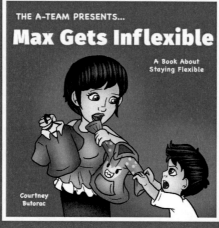

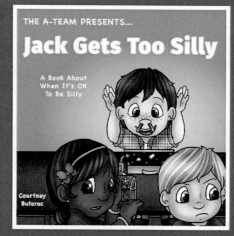

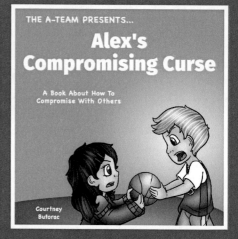

Made in the USA
San Bernardino, CA
05 May 2019